Value Guide
for
IMPERIAL GLASS

by

Margaret & Douglas Archer

$2.00

COLLECTOR BOOKS
P.O. Box 3009
Paducah, Kentucky 42001

VALUE GUIDE

Value Guides have always been controversial. This one will be no different. We can only present what we believe to be a fair value that would average out for any section of the country. Therefore, we have listed a low and high retail value that gives a price range for everyone. As stated above, this is only a guide and should be used as such. Any differences of opinion are welcome, as we can only improve our knowledge from the help of others and pricing is no exception.

Margaret & Douglas Archer

CATALOG 100F
LAMP SHADES

Page 3
Shades:

S-601/2	5.00-7.00
S-561/2	6.00-8.00
S-559/2	7.00-9.00
0279	5.00-7.00
551	5.00-7.00

Page 4
Shades:

S-601/6	5.00-7.00
S-591/6	6.00-8.00
S-583/6	6.00-8.00
S-601/38	5.00-7.00
S-591/38	6.00-8.00
S-583/38	6.00-8.00

Page 5
Shades:

0591/37	5.00-7.00
0583/37	6.00-8.00
0559/33	5.00-7.00
S-561/39	5.00-7.00
S-561/34	5.00-7.00
S-561/40	5.00-7.00

Page 6
Shades:

0553/31	15.00-18.00
0544/31	12.00-14.00
0553/232	15.00-18.00
0544/232	12.00-14.00

Page 7
Shades:

0591/36	5.00-7.00
0583/36	6.00-8.00
0561/35	5.00-7.00
0601/35	5.00-7.00
0591/35	5.00-7.00
0583/35	6.00-8.00

Page 8
Shades:

S-544- 6 Stars	12.00-13.00
S-544-12 Stars	13.00-14.00
S-544-18 Stars	14.00-16.00
S-559- 6 Stars	10.00-11.00
S-559- 9 Stars	11.00-12.00
S-559-12 Stars	12.00-13.00

Page 9

Shades:

S-601-4 Stars 10.00-12.00
S-561-4 Stars 10.00-12.00
S-559-6 Stars 14.00-16.00
S-279/102 . . . . .18.00-20.00
S-551/1029 . . . . .16.00-18.00

Page 10

Shades:

S-544/103 . . . . .16.00-18.00
S-591/103 . . . . .12.00-14.00
S-601/103 . . . . .10.00-12.00
S-583/103 . . . . .13.00-15.00
S-552/103 . . . . .16.00-18.00
S-548/103 . . . . .16.00-18.00

Page 11

Shades:

S-601/104 . . . . .8.00-10.00
S-561/104 . . . . .8.00-10.00
S-559/104 . . . . .12.00-14.00
S-551/104 . . . . .12.00-14.00
S-279/104 . . . . .16.00-18.00

Page 12

Shades:

S-554/105 . . . . .16.00-18.00
S-535/105 . . . . .16.00-18.00
S-591/105 . . . . .12.00-14.00
S-583/105 . . . . .13.00-15.00
S-548/105 . . . . .16.00-18.00
S-552/105 . . . . .16.00-18.00

Page 13

Shades:

S-544/1064 . . . . .14.00-16.00
S-544/1066 . . . . .15.00-17.00
S-535/106 . . . . .14.00-16.00
S-591/106 . . . . .14.00-16.00
S-601/106 . . . . .10.00-12.00
S-561/106 . . . . .10.00-12.00

Page 14

Shades:

358½C-Gas 20.00-24.00
358½C-Electric 16.00-18.00
359½B-Gas 18.00-22.00
359½B-Electric 14.00-16.00
359½C-Gas 20.00-24.00
359½C-Electric 14.00-16.00

Page 15

Shades:

342½C-Electric 16.00-18.00
342½C-Gas 20.00-24.00
486C-Electric 16.00-18.00
486C-Gas 20.00-24.00
474C-Electric 16.00-18.00
474C-Gas 20.00-24.00

Page 16

Shades:

430C-Gas 18.00-20.00
430C-Electric 14.00-16.00
430B-Gas 16.00-18.00
430B-Electric 12.00-14.00
48C-Gas 20.00-24.00
48C-Electric 16.00-18.00

Page 17

Shades:

49½-Electric 18.00-20.00
49½-Gas 22.00-24.00
45½C-Electric 18.00-20.00
45½-Gas 24.00-26.00
46C-Electric 20.00-22.00
46C-Gas 24.00-28.00

Page 18

Shades:

279C-Gas 16.00-18.00
279C-Electric 12.00-14.00
255C-Gas 18.00-20.00
255C-Electric 14.00-16.00

Page 19

Shades:

255/10-Electric 14.00-16.00
255/10-Gas 18.00-20.00
255/4-Electric 14.00-16.00
255/4-Gas 18.00-20.00
255C/2Electric 14.00-16.00
255C/2Gas 18.00-20.00

Page 20

Smoke Shades:

54-7" .10.00-12.00
054-7" 10.00-12.00
47-6" 8.00-12.00
47-7" .10.00-12.00
47-8" .12.00-14.00
047-6" 10.00-12.00
047-7" 12.00-14.00
047-8" 16.00-18.00

Continued on Page 4

Continued from Page 3

252-6" 8.00-12.00
252-7" 10.00-12.00
252-8" 12.00-14.00
0252-6" 10.00-12.00
0252-7" 12.00-14.00
0252-8" 16.00-18.00

CATALOG 104F

Page 22

Berry-283A 18.00-22.00
Berry-283C 20.00-24.00
Table Set-2831 ....80.00-90.00
   Butter & Cover 25.00-30.00
   Sugar & Cover 25.00-30.00
   Cream 10.00-14.00
   Spoon 10.00-14.00

Page 23

Pitcher-283 ....25.00-35.00
Pitcher-2831 ....30.00-37.00
Pitcher-2832 ....32.00-38.00
Pitcher-281A 35.00-40.00
Tumbler-281A 8.00-10.00
Tumbler-2831 ....6.00-8.00
Tumbler-283 ....6.00-8.00

Page 24

Compote-274B 14.00-16.00
Compote-274C 14.00-16.00
Table Set-274 ....55.00-60.00
   Butter & Cover 18.00-20.00
   Sugar & Cover 18.00-20.00
   Cream 8.00-10.00
   Spoon 8.00-10.00

Page 25

Compote-274A-4½" 10.00-12.00
Compote-274A-8" 14.00-16.00
Celery-Tall-274 ....20.00-24.00
Table Set-302 ....65.00-70.00
   Butter & Cover 20.00-22.00
   Sugar & Cover 20.00-22.00
   Cream 10.00-14.00
   Spoon 10.00-14.00

Page 26

Nut Bowl-2461N 8.00-10.00
Nut Bowl-2461P 12.00-14.00
Banana Dish-2461E 16.00-20.00
Compote-2461A 10.00-12.00
Grape Dish-2461C 12.00-14.00
Celery Boat-2461M 12.00-14.00

Page 27

Salver-2461D 20.00-22.00
Card Receiver-2461R 20.00-22.00
Berry-276A 18.00-20.00
Berry-276C 16.00-18.00
Ice Cream Dish-2461F 14.00-18.00
Nut Bowl-276N 15.00-17.00
Plate-276D 22.00-24.00

Page 28

Berry-88B 12.00-14.00
Berry-88C 4½" 10.00-12.00
Berry-88C 7" 14.00-16.00
Plate-88D 6" 16.00-18.00
Plate-88D 10" 20.00-24.00
Celery Boat-46E 24.00-28.00
Banana Dish-46M 24.00-28.00

Page 29

Plate-89D-10" 18.00-20.00
Ice Cream Plate-46D 14.00-16.00
Berry-89B-4" 8.00-10.00
Berry-89B-7" 10.00-12.00
Berry-89C-4" 8.00-10.00
Berry-89C-7" 10.00-12.00
Grape Dish-46C 20.00-24.00
Nut Bowl-46N 14.00-16.00

Page 30

Berry-47A 10.00-12.00
Nut Bowl-47N 8.00-10.00
Plate-47D-10" 12.00-14.00
Celery Boat-47E 14.00-18.00
Berry-263-4½" 6.00-8.00
Berry-263-7" 8.00-10.00
Berry-263-8" 10.00-12.00
Cucumber Dish-280 ....12.00-14.00

Page 31

Berry-47B 14.00-16.00
Berry-47C 10.00-12.00
Radish Dish-293 ....16.00-20.00
Sugar & Cover-272 ....16.00-18.00
Oil Bottle-277 ....17.00-19.00
Oil Bottle-286 ....15.00-18.00
Pitcher-300 ....30.00-35.00
Tumbler-300 ....8.00-10.00
Brandy Bottle-40 ....20.00-22.00

Page 32

Compote-6-4½"	8.00-12.00
Compote-6-8"	10.00-16.00
Water Bottle-099A	14.00-16.00
Oil Bottle-099A	18.00-20.00
Salt Shaker-286A	4.00-5.00
Salt Shaker-286A	4.00-5.00
Lemonade Set-232	25.00-30.00

Page 33

Molasses Can-69A	15.00-18.00
Molasses Can-69A	15.00-18.00
Molasses Can-69A	15.00-18.00
Molasses Can-69A	15.00-18.00
Sugar Shaker-68A Flat Top	6.00-8.00
Sugar Shaker-68A	10.00-12.00
Berry-6-4½"	8.00-12.00
Berry-6-8"	10.00-16.00
Lemonade Set-083A	25.00-30.00

Page 34

Molasses Can-286 (Common Top)	15.00-18.00
Molasses Can-286 (Tin Top)	18.00-20.00
Molasses Can-286 (Nickle Top)	22.00-24.00
Molasses Can-286 (Silver Top)	30.00-34.00
Salt-291	3.00-4.00
Sugar Duster-286 (Flat Top)	6.00-8.00
Sugar Duster-286 (Silver Top)	8.00-10.00
Salt-286 (Silver Top)	4.00-6.00
Salt-286 (Dome Top)	3.00-4.00
Salt-286 (Flat Top)	3.00-4.00
Sugar Shaker-337	10.00-12.00
Water Bottle-287	12.00-14.00
Pitcher-84B	18.00-20.00

Page 35

Pitcher-83A	18.00-20.00
Pitcher-299	18.00-20.00
Pitcher-82A	18.00-20.00
Pitcher-289	18.00-20.00

Page 36

Bonquet-246A	8.00-10.00
Bonquet-246B	8.00-10.00
Bonquet-246C	8.00-10.00
Violet Holder-246D	7.00-9.00
Violet Holder-294H	10.00-12.00
Vase-294	14.00-16.00
Vase-2461A	9.00-11.00
Vase-2461C	9.00-11.00
Rose Bowl-2461N	9.00-11.00
Sweet Pea Holder-284E	10.00-12.00

Page 37

Sweet Pea Holder-284A-8"	8.00-10.00
Sweet Pea Holder-284A-10"	10.00-12.00
Sweet Pea Holder-284E	10.00-12.00
Vase-284-12"	12.00-14.00
Vase-284-16"	14.00-16.00
Rose Bowl-284H	12.00-14.00

Page 38

Table Set-256	70.00-80.00
Butter & Cover	20.00-23.00
Sugar & Cover	20.00-23.00
Cream	10.00-14.00
Spoon	10.00-14.00
Oil Bottle-256	14.00-16.00
Salt-256	4.00-6.00
Bouquet-256	8.00-10.00
Plate-2566D	10.00-12.00
Berry-256U	5.00-7.00
Plate-256D	8.00-9.00

Page 39

Berry-2567A	8.00-10.00
Berry-2567B	8.00-10.00
Berry-2567C	9.00-11.00
Berry-2567S	10.00-12.00
Berry-2567W	8.00-10.00
Nappy Ice Cream-2567F	10.00-12.00
Nut Bowl-2567N	8.00-10.00
Casserole-2567	9.00-11.00

Page 40

Celery Boat-2567E	14.00-16.00
Pear Bowl-2567P	10.00-12.00
Lemonade Set-256	30.00-35.00

Page 41

Berry-2826A	10.00-14.00
Berry-2826C	12.00-14.00
Berry-2826S	14.00-16.00
Nut Bowl-2826N	8.00-9.00
Pear Bowl-2826P	8.00-10.00
Ice Cream-2826F	10.00-12.00
Banana Dish-2826O	12.00-14.00

Page 42

Berry-2823C	4.00-6.00
Berry-2824C	5.00-7.00
Berry-2825C	6.00-8.00
Berry-2827C	8.00-10.00
Orange Bowl-2829C	10.00-12.00
Banana Dish-2829O	14.00-16.00
Banana Dish-2827O	13.00-15.00
Spoon Tray-2825O	8.00-10.00
Spoon Tray-2820	14.00-18.00

Page 43

Plate-2829R	14.00-16.00
Plate-2829D	14.00-16.00
Plate-2824D	8.00-10.00
Plate-2825D	9.00-11.00
Green Onion Dish-2824E	8.00-10.00
Green Onion Dish-2825E	10.00-12.00

Page 44

Berry-2820A	8.00-9.00
Bon Bon-2820B	8.00-10.00
Bon Bon-2820P	7.00-9.00
Bon Bon-2825P	8.00-10.00
Grape Dish-2829H	12.00-14.00
Olive Dish-2820C	8.00-10.00
Olive Dish-2820S	8.00-10.00
Custard-282	4.00-8.00
Pear Bowl-2827P	8.00-10.00
Ice Cream Dish-282F	20.00-26.00

Page 45

Bowl-282A	20.00-26.00
Bowl-282B	20.00-26.00
Jelly-2822A	5.00-6.00
Jelly-2822B	5.00-6.00
Jelly-2822C	6.00-8.00
Card Plate-2822D	7.00-9.00

Page 46

Pitcher-282	14.00-16.00
Pitcher-282B	15.00-18.00
Brandy Bottle-282	18.00-20.00
Whiskey Bottle-282	18.00-20.00
Tumbler-282	3.00-4.00
Whiskey Glass	2.00-3.00
Wine Glass-282	3.00-4.00
Goblet-282	4.00-5.00

Page 47

Vase-282B	12.00-16.00
Oil Bottle	14.00-16.00
Molasses Can-282	16.00-18.00
Salt-282	6.00-8.00
Lily Bowl-2827J	8.00-10.00
Wine Set	60.00-70.00

Page 48

Cracker Jar-282	24.00-30.00
Milk Jar-282	20.00-24.00
Celery-282	16.00-18.00
Table Set-282	70.00-80.00
Butter & Cover	20.00-24.00
Sugar & Cover	20.00-24.00
Cream	10.00-12.00
Spoon	10.00-12.00

Page 49

Table Set-292	90.00-100.00
Butter & Cover	24.00-28.00
Sugar & Cover	24.00-28.00
Cream	14.00-18.00
Spoon	14.00-18.00

Page 50

Pitcher-Small-292	14.00-18.00
Pitcher-Large-292	18.00-24.00
Sugar-2927A	14.00-16.00
Sugar-2927S	14.00-18.00
Cream-2927A	14.00-18.00
Cream-2927S	14.00-18.00
Tumbler-292	8.00-12.00
Spoon-292	16.00-18.00

Page 51

Rose Bowl-2921N	8.00-12.00
Rose Bowl-2922N	9.00-12.00
Sherbet-2921A	8.00-12.00
Jelly-2922A	9.00-14.00
Vase-2925A	9.00-12.00
Vase-2925B	10.00-12.00
Vase-2925E	10.00-12.00
Punch Bowl-292	16.00-18.00
Custard-292	6.00-8.00

CATALOG 101D

Page 54

Nut Bowl-5927N/115	12.00-14.00
Jug-84/115	30.00-40.00

Page 55

Tumbler-84/102	6.00-7.00
Ice Tea-84/102	8.00-9.00
Ice Tea-84/102 & Plate	14.00-16.00
Vase or Celery-572/102	10.00-12.00
Salt-268/102	6.00-8.00
Syrup-286/102 7 ½ oz.	14.00-16.00
Syrup-286/102 12oz.	16.00-18.00
Syrup-69/102	18.00-20.00

Page 56

Nut Bowl-5925N/102	8.00-10.00
Nut Bowl-5926N/102	10.00-12.00
Plate-84/102	6.00-8.00
Salad Bowl-5735B/102	12.00-14.00
Salad Bowl-5737B/102	14.00-16.00

Page 57

Jug-84/110-Pint	30.00-36.00
Jug-84/110-Quart	34.00-40.00
Jug-84/110-3 Pint	36.00-42.00
Jug-84/110-3 Quart	38.00-46.00
Jug-84/110-½ Gal	40.00-50.00

Page 58

Plate 84/110	8.00-10.00
Nut Bowl-5926N/110	10.00-12.00
Candy Bowl-57835N/110	12.00-14.00
Salad Bowl-5735B/110	14.00-16.00
Salad Bowl-5737B/110	16.00-18.00

Page 59

Plate-84/112	7.00-9.00
Nut Bowl-5926N/112	9.00-11.00
Salad Bowl-5735B/112	13.00-17.00
Salad Bowl-5737B/112	15.00-18.00

Page 60

Tumbler-84/113	7.00-9.00
Ice Tea-84/113	9.00-11.00
Ice Tea & Plate-84/113	18.00-20.00
Vase or Celery-572/113	12.00-14.00
Salt-286/113	8.00-10.00
Syrup Can-286/113 7 ½ oz.	16.00-18.00
Syrup Can-286/113 12oz.	18.00-20.00
Syrup Can-69/113	20.00-24.00

Page 61

Plate-84/113	8.00-10.00
Nut Bowl-5926N/113	10.00-12.00
Salad Bowl-5735B/113	14.00-16.00
Salad Bowl-5737B/113	16.00-18.00

Page 62

Plate-84/114	8.00-10.00
Nut Bowl-5926N/114	10.00-12.00
Salad Bowl-5737B/114	14.00-16.00
Salad Bowl-5737B/114	16.00-18.00

Page 63

Berry-5927A/114	14.00-16.00
Berry-5924A/114	6.00-8.00
Berry-5924 ½ A/114	8.00-10.00
Berry-5925A/114	16.00-18.00
Berry-5928A/114	10.00-12.00

Page 64

Tumbler-090/300	6.00-7.00
Ice Tea-84/300	8.00-9.00
Ice Tea & Plate-84/300	14.00-16.00
Vase or Celery-572/300	10.00-12.00
Salt-286/300	6.00-8.00
Molasses Can-286/300 7 ½ oz.	14.00-16.00
Molasses Can-286/300 12 oz.	16.00-18.00
Molasses Can-69/300	18.00-20.00

Page 65

Plate-84/300	8.00-10.00
Finger Bowl-84/300	6.00-8.00
Custard-91/300	4.00-6.00
Sherbert-108/300	4.00-6.00
Sundae-208/300	5.00-7.00
Jelly-209/300	6.00-8.00
Ice Cream-1081/300	4.00-6.00
Ice Cream-208/300	5.00-7.00
Ice Cream-2091/300	6.00-8.00

Page 66

Olive Bowl-6065/300	6.00-8.00
Sugar-606/300	6.00-8.00
Cream-606/300	6.00-8.00
Bon Bon-6025/300	6.00-8.00
Pickle Dish-84/300	8.00-10.00
Bowl-Footed-6067B/300	16.00-20.00

Page 67

Jug-84/301-Pint	28.00-34.00
Jug-84/301-Quart	30.00-36.00
Jug-84/301-3 Pint	34.00-40.00
Jug-84/301-3 Quart	36.00-44.00
Jug-84/301-½ Gal	38.00-48.00

Page 68

Plate-84/301	9.00-11.00
Custard-91/301	5.00-7.00
Finger Bowl-84/301	7.00-9.00
Sherbert-108/301	5.00-7.00
Sundae-208/301	6.00-8.00
Jelly-209/301	7.00-9.00
Ice Cream-1081/301	5.00-7.00
Ice Cream-2081/301	6.00-8.00
Ice Cream-2091/301	7.00-9.00

Page 69

Olive-6065/301	7.00-9.00
Sugar-606/301	7.00-9.00
Cream-606/301	7.00-9.00
Bon Bon-60251/301	7.00-9.00
Pickle Dish-84/301	9.00-11.00
Bowl-Footed-6067B/301	18.00-20.00

Page 70

Olive-6065	5.00-7.00
Sugar-606	5.00-7.00
Cream-606	5.00-7.00
Bon Bon-60251	5.00-7.00
Pickle Dish-84	7.00-9.00
Bowl-Footed-6067B	14.00-16.00

Page 71

Ice Tea-515A	3.00-4.00
Ice Tea-515B	3.00-4.00

Continued on Page 8

Tumbler-515A 4.00-5.00
Tumbler-515B 4.00-5.00
Jug-0515 . . . . 22.00-26.00
Jug-515 . . . . 18.00-20.00

Page 72
Mayonnaise & Plate-05825 . . . . 10.00-12.00
Salad Bowl & Plate-05826 . . . . 12.00-14.00
Tumbler-0582 . . . . 4.00-6.00
Jug-5821 . . . . 25.00-30.00
Tumbler (Bell) 05821 . . . . 5.00-7.00

Page 73
Salt (Open) 582 . . . . 6.00-8.00
Bowl-582 . . . . 10.00-12.00
Water Bottle-5822 . . . . 12.00-14.00
Water Bottle-05822 . . . . 16.00-18.00

Page 74
Salt or Pepper-582 . . . . 6.00-8.00
Oil Bottle-5821 . . . . 14.00-18.00
Oil Bottle-5822 . . . . 14.00-18.00
Oil Bottle-05821 . . . . 18.00-22.00
Oil Bottle-05822 . . . . 18.00-22.00

Page 75
Butter & Cover-05821 . . . . 20.00-30.00
Berry-582 . . . . 10.00-12.00
Bread & Butter Plate-582 . . . . 8.00-10.00
Bread & Butter Plate-5822D 12.00-14.00

Page 76
Vase-582 . . . . 7.00-9.00
Sugar (Hotel)-582 . . . . 6.00-8.00
Cream (Hotel)-582 . . . . 6.00-8.00
Vase-Sweet Pea-5822-7" 9.00-11.00
Vase-Rose-5822-10" 10.00-12.00
Vase-Flower-5822-12" 12.00-14.00

Page 77
Sugar & Cover-0582 . . . . 10.00-14.00
Cream-0582 . . . . 6.00-8.00
Butter & Cover-0582 . . . . 12.00-16.00
Spoon-0582 . . . . 6.00-8.00

BARGAIN BOOK

Page 83
Vase-412-22 . . . . 90.00-100.00
Vase-417-30 . . . . 55.00-60.00
Vase-418-10 . . . . 40.00-50.00
Vase-618-12 . . . . 70.00-80.00
Vase-419-22 . . . . 90.00-100.00

Page 84
Vase-413-14 . . . . 60.00-70.00
Vase-418-12 . . . . 90.00-100.00
Vase-419-44 . . . . 70.00-80.00
Vase-622-11 . . . . 40.00-50.00
Vase-623-21 . . . . 50.00-60.00

Page 85
Vase-415-11 . . . . 50.00-60.00
Vase-417-20 . . . . 55.00-60.00
Vase-618-10 . . . . 40.00-50.00
Vase-622-21 . . . . 50.00-60.00
Vase-623-40 . . . . 40.00-50.00

Page 86
Vase-618 . . . . 70.00-80.00
Vase-619 . . . . 90.00-100.00
Vase-622 . . . . 70.00-80.00
Vase-655 . . . . 70.00-80.00

Page 87
Vase-412 . . . . 50.00-60.00
Vase-412 . . . . 70.00-80.00
Vase-417 . . . . 55.00-65.00
Vase-417 . . . . 70.00-80.00
Vase-623 . . . . 50.00-60.00
Vase-623 . . . . 70.00-80.00

Page 88
Vase-413 . . . . 70.00-80.00
Vase-413 . . . . 90.00-100.00
Vase-643 . . . . 50.00-60.00
Vase-643 . . . . 80.00-90.00
Rose Bowl-3761 . . . . 50.00-60.00
Rose Bowl-3761 . . . . 70.00-80.00

Page 89
Vase-415 . . . . 50.00-60.00
Vase-418 . . . . 100.00-120.00
Vase-419 . . . . 90.00-100.00

Page 90
Console Set 60.00-70.00
    Bowl-3762 . . . . 20.00-30.00
    Vases (Pair)-319 . . . . 30.00-40.00
Console Set 40.00-50.00
    Bowl-376 . . . . 15.00-20.00
    Vases (Pair)-319 . . . . 20.00-30.00

Page 91
Vase-415/95 . . . . 30.00-40.00
Vase-418/94 . . . . 35.00-45.00
Vase-419/95 . . . . 30.00-40.00
Rose Vase-618/93 . . . . 25.00-30.00
Bud Vase-619/93 . . . . 20.00-25.00
Vase-622/93 . . . . 20.00-25.00
Vase-655/93 . . . . 25.00-30.00

Page 92

Vase-119/99	20.00-25.00
Vase-729/12	25.00-30.00
Vase-731/98	25.00-30.00
Vase-223/12	35.00-40.00
Vase-768/12	35.00-40.00
Vase-771/12	30.00-35.00

Page 93

Handled Fruit Bowl-6641/12	18.00-20.00
Handled Fruit Bowl-6641/30	18.00-20.00
Sandwich Tray-664/12	16.00-18.00
Sandwich Tray-664/30	16.00-18.00

Page 94

Sandwich Tray-664/7	10.00-12.00
Sandwich Tray-664/10	10.00-12.00
Cheese & Cracker Set-641/7	8.00-10.00
Cheese & Cracker Set-641/10	8.00-10.00

Page 95

Sandwich Tray-664/20	10.00-12.00
Sandwich Tray-664/13	10.00-12.00
Cheese & Cracker Set-641/20	8.00-10.00
Cheese & Cracker Set-641/13	8.00-10.00

Page 96

Salad Plate-645D/10(Ea.)	2.00-3.00
Salad Plate & Bowl	9.00-11.00
Plate-648D/7	3.00-4.00
Bowl-648B/7	4.00-5.00

Page 97

Salad Plate-645D/20 (Ea.)	2.00-3.00
Salad Plate & Bowl	9.00-11.00
Plate-648D/13	3.00-4.00
Bowl-648B/13	4.00-5.00

Page 98

Salad Plate-2428/2	2.00-3.00
Salad Plate-2428/7	2.00-3.00
Salad Plate-2428/20	2.00-3.00
Salad Plate-2428/30	2.00-3.00
Salad Plate-2428/57	2.00-3.00
Salad Plate-2428/88	2.00-3.00

Page 99

Candlestick-6247/61	5.00-7.00
Candlestick-6249/63	7.00-9.00
Candlestick-62412/66	8.00-10.00
Night Set-650/57	10.00-12.00
Night Set-650/88	10.00-12.00

Page 100

Ice Tea-803/20	2.00-3.00
Ice Tea-803/88	2.00-3.00
Ice Tea-803/90	2.00-3.00
Jug-84/88	10.00-12.00
Jug-599/20	10.00-12.00
Jug-599/90	10.00-12.00

Page 101

Sugar-606/20	4.00-6.00
Cream-606/20	4.00-6.00
Nappy-846/20	5.00-7.00
Lily Bowl-6567/20N	4.00-6.00
Basket-300/20	10.00-12.00
Oil Bottle-625/20	14.00-18.00
Salad-6567/20B	5.00-7.00
Celery Tray-6150/20	5.00-7.00

Page 102

Sugar-615/28	4.00-6.00
Cream-615/28	4.00-6.00
Nappy-6674/28	4.00-6.00
Bon Bon-6151/28	5.00-6.00
Sherbet-499A/28	2.00-3.00
Sherbet Plate-499/28	2.00-3.00
Nappy-6154½/28	2.00-3.00
Pickle-615/28	5.00-7.00

Page 103

Berry-5145A	18.00-20.00
Berry-5145C	20.00-22.00
Berry-4735A	16.00-18.00
Berry-4735C	18.00-20.00
Berry-4895A	18.00-20.00
Berry-4895C	20.00-22.00
Berry-2565/3C	16.00-18.00
Bowl-Footed-600B	12.00-14.00

Page 104

Berry-L2567/3C	24.00-28.00
Salad Bowl-M465	30.00-34.00
Berry-K7007/4A	22.00-26.00
Berry-K4897A	20.00-24.00
Berry-M496C	26.00-30.00

Page 105

Salad Bowl-4891A	32.00-36.00
Salad Bowl-5141C	28.00-32.00
Fruit Bowl-4898C	30.00-32.00
Fruit Bowl-4738A	30.00-32.00

Page 106

Fruit Bowl-5141F	18.00-24.00
Salad or Flower Bowl-5141N.C.	20.00-22.00
Fruit Bowl-4892B	30.00-32.00
Fruit Bowl-4892C	30.00-32.00

Page 107

Candlestick (Pair)-6007	18.00-24.00
Salad Bowl-5141/2B	30.00-34.00
Candlestick (Pair)-635	42.00-46.00
Bowl-6567/2B	18.00-20.00
Bowl Base-634	6.00-8.00

Page 108

Candlestick (Pair)-635	42.00-46.00
Bowl-6569/2B	18.00-20.00
Plate-6569/2D	8.00-10.00

Page 109

Salad Set	40.00-50.00
Plate-805D (Single)	4.00-6.00
Bowl-808B	8.00-10.00
Plate-808D	4.00-6.00

Page 110

Salad Set	60.00-70.00
Plate-645/2D (Single)	6.00-8.00
Bowl-647/2B	10.00-12.00
Plate-647/2D	8.00-10.00

Page 111

Basket-300	10.00-12.00
Basket-698	14.00-16.00
Sundae Set	40.00-50.00
Bowl-3457B	10.00-12.00
Sherbet-499/1B (Single)	4.00-5.00

Page 112

Rose Bowl-769 & Plate-641	18.00-20.00
Salad Bowl-6567/2B	30.00-36.00
Sherbet-6001B	4.00-5.00
Plate-6724D	4.00-5.00

Page 113

Fruit Bowl-6641	18.00-20.0
Salad Plate-6724D	8.00-10.00
Sandwich Tray-664	16.00-18.00
Cheese & Cracker Set	18.00-20.00

Page 114

Vase-477	28.00-32.00
Vase-480	25.00-30.00
Vase-488	30.00-34.00

Page 115

Candlestick-41	12.00-14.00
Candlestick-635	20.00-24.00
Candlestick-419	14.00-16.00
Vase-710	8.00-10.00
Vase-682	8.00-10.00
Vase-711	8.00-10.00

Page 116

Spoon-M489	18.00-20.00
Sugar & Cover-M489	26.00-30.00
Cream-M489	20.00-22.00
Berry-M4895A	18.00-20.00
Butter & Cover-M489	30.00-36.00
Tumbler-M489	8.00-10.00
Berry-M4898A	30.00-32.00
Pitcher-M489	32.00-36.00

Page 117

Wine-473	6.00-8.00
Cup & Saucer-473	12.00-14.00
Wine Set:	70.00-80.00
Wine Bottle-473	32.00-36.00
Wine Glass (Single) 473	6.00-8.00

Page 118

Water Sets:

Pitcher-M484	36.00-40.00
Tumbler-M484	8.00-10.00
Pitcher-M5143	40.00-46.00
Tumbler-M514	10.00-14.00
Pitcher-M6783	40.00-48.00
Tumbler-M678	10.00-14.00
Pitcher-M4743	38.00-42.00
Tumbler-M474	8.00-10.00

Page 119

Jug-5142	36.00-40.00
Jug-494	36.00-40.00
Water Set-473	
Pitcher	34.00-38.00
Tumbler	8.00-10.00

Page 120

Table Salt (Open)-M600	6.00-8.00
Tooth Pick-M600	8.00-10.00
Sherbet-M600	8.00-10.00
Ice Cream M-M6001	9.00-11.00
Sherbet-M399/1	8.00-10.00
Custard-M755/1	6.00-8.00
Custard-M672	8.00-10.00
Ice Cream & Plate-M666	14.00-18.00
Cup & Saucer-M5822B	12.00-14.00
Child's Mug-M593	14.00-16.00
Cafe Parfait-M5823	12.00-14.00
Ice Cream & Plate-M632	20.00-26.00
Lemonade Glass-7600	16.00-20.00

Page 121

Cordial-M442/1	4.00-5.00
Wine-M442/1 2oz.	4.00-5.00
Wine-M442/1 3oz.	5.00-6.00
Claret-M442/1	6.00-7.00

Continued on Page 11

Continued from Page 10

Champagne-M442/1 . . . . .7.00-8.00
Goblet-M442/1 9 oz. 8.00-9.00
Goblet-M442/ 10 oz 9.00-10.00
Cordial-M666 . . . . .4.00-5.00
Wine-M666 . . . . .5.00-6.00
Goblet-M666 . . . . .7.00-9.00
Wine-M9 1 ½ oz. 4.00-5.00
Wine-M9 3oz. 5.00-6.00
Claret-M9 . . . . .7.00-8.00
Goblet-M9 . . . . .9.00-10.00

Page 122

Sugar-682 . . . . .10.00-12.00
Cream-682 . . . . .10.00-12.00
Compote-682 . . . . .18.00-20.00
Celery Tray-682 . . . . .18.00-20.00

Page 123

Sugar-711 . . . . .4.00-6.00
Creamer-711 . . . . .4.00-6.00
Olive-711 . . . . .4.00-6.00
Jelly-711 . . . . .5.00-7.00
Sherbet-7111 . . . . .4.00-6.00
Berry-7115A 5.00-6.00
Berry-7115B 5.00-6.00

Page 124

Butter & Cover-671 . . . . .12.00-14.00
Sugar & Cover-671 . . . . .8.00-10.00
Cream-671 . . . . .4.00-5.00
Spoon-671 . . . . .5.00-6.00
Celery-671 . . . . .8.00-9.00
Milk Pitcher-671 . . . . .10.00-12.00

Page 125

Nappy-7105B 5.00-6.00
Lily Bowl-7105N .5.00-6.00
Sugar-710 . . . . .4.00-5.00
Cream-710 . . . . .4.00-5.00
Berry-710 . . . . .5.00-6.00
Celery Tray-710 . . . . .6.00-8.00
Pickle Dish-710 . . . . .7.00-9.00
Olive-710 . . . . .5.00-6.00

Page 126

Nappy-7106A 5.00-7.00
Salad Bowl-7106B 6.00-8.00
Lily Bowl-7106N .5.00-6.00
Jelly Dish-710 . . . . .5.00-8.00
Compote-710B 7.00-9.00
Square Dish & Plate-710 . . . . .10.00-12.00
Jug-710 . . . . .9.00-12.00

Page 127

Berry-7117A 6.00-8.00
Berry-6987A 7.00-9.00
Berry-6827A 7.00-9.00
Salad-7117B 7.00-9.00
Salad-6987B 7.00-10.00
Salad-6827B 7.00-10.00

Page 128

Berry Dish-7114B 4.00-5.00
Berry Bowl-7118B 8.00-9.00
Berry Bowl-6828B 9.00-10.00
Berry Dish-6824B 4.00-5.00
Berry Dish-5824B 5.00-7.00
Berry Bowl-5828B 9.00-11.00

Page 129

Sugar-595 . . . . .4.00-5.00
Cream-595 . . . . .4.00-5.00
Sugar-588 . . . . .3.00-4.00
Cream-588 . . . . .3.00-4.00
Sugar-609/1 . . . . .3.00-4.00
Cream-609/1 . . . . .3.00-4.00
Sherbet & Plate-499/1B 4.00-5.00
Sherbet & Plate-60003/6724 . . . . .4.00-5.00
Sherbet & Plate-499B 4.00-5.00

Page 130

Square Bowl & Plate-698 . . . . .10.00-12.00
Sugar & Cover-698 . . . . .8.00-10.00
Cream-698 . . . . .4.00-5.00
Spoon-698 . . . . .5.00-6.00
Butter & Cover-698 . . . . .12.00-14.00

Page 131

Water Set 30.00-34.00
    Pitcher-7113 . . . . .10.00-12.00
    Tumbler-711 (Single) 2.00-2.50
Water Set 34.00-36.00
    Pitcher-06003 . . . . .14.00-16.00
    Tumbler-672 (Single) 2.00-2.50

Page 132

Jug-310 . . . . .6.00-8.00
Graduated Jug-321 . . . . .7.00-9.00
Candy Jar & Cover-711 . . . . .10.00-12.00
Vase-698 . . . . .8.00-10.00

BOOK "E"

Page 135

Berry-212/8 . . . . 8.00-10.00
Spoon Tray-212/6 . . . . 10.00-12.00
Pickle-212/7 . . . . 9.00-11.00
Olive-212/9 . . . . 7.00-9.00
Nappy-212/5 . . . . 6.00-8.00
Compote-212/10 . . . . 12.00-14.00
Berry-212/3 . . . . 6.00-8.00
Sugar-212/1 . . . . 6.00-8.00
Cream-212/2 . . . . 6.00-8.00
Vase-212/11 . . . . 8.00-10.00

Page 136

Punch Set-SNAP 14 . . . . 60.00-70.00
   Bowl & Foot 30.00-40.00
   Cup (Single) 4.00-5.00

Page 137

Ice Tea-586A 4.00-5.00
Ice Tea-586B 4.00-5.00
Tumbler-586A 4.00-5.00
Tumbler-586B 4.00-5.00
Tankard-586 . . . . 14.00-16.00

Page 138

Vase-282C 20.00-25.00
Vase-Handled-2821 . . . . 30.00-35.00
Lemonade Set-282 . . . . 60.00-70.00
   Glass Tray-2829 . . . . 10.00-12.00
   Pitcher-282 . . . . 10.00-12.00
   Tumbler-282 (Single) 5.00-6.00

Page 139

Fern Dish (with Lining)-587 . . . . 20.00-25.00
Fern Dish-587 . . . . 16.00-18.00

Page 140

Nappy-541 . . . . 10.00-12.00
Pickle-495 . . . . 12.00-14.00
Spoon Tray-539 . . . . 8.00-10.00
Compote-574 . . . . 12.00-14.00
Square Nappy-576 . . . . 8.00-10.00
Berry-453 . . . . 6.00-8.00
Sugar-526 . . . . 6.00-8.00
Cream-526 . . . . 6.00-8.00

Page 141

Nappy-499/6A 9.00-11.00
Celery Tray-466 . . . . 8.00-10.00
Compote-485/1 . . . . 10.00-12.00
Berry-517 . . . . 8.00-10.00
Salad-504 . . . . 8.00-10.00
Vase-529 . . . . 12.00-14.00

Page 142

Salad-534/9F 15.00-17.00
Salad-502 . . . . 10.00-12.00
Salad-464 . . . . 12.00-14.00
Footed Oval-607 . . . . 14.00-16.00

Page 143

Berry-212/8 . . . . 8.00-10.00
Nappy-212/5 . . . . 6.00-8.00
Vase-212/11 . . . . 8.00-10.00
Compote-212/10 . . . . 12.00-14.00
Cream-212/2 . . . . 6.00-8.00
Sugar-212/1 . . . . 6.00-8.00
Olive-212/9 . . . . 7.00-9.00
Pickle-212/7 . . . . 9.00-11.00

Page 144

Nappy-555A 8.00-10.00
Spoon Tray-555 . . . . 12.00-14.00
Square Nappy-555S 8.00-10.00
Bon Bon-555 . . . . 6.00-8.00
Jelly-555 . . . . 9.00-11.00
Pickle-555 . . . . 6.00-8.00
Vase-536 . . . . 6.00-8.00
Sugar-555 . . . . 6.00-8.00
Cream-555 . . . . 6.00-8.00

Page 145

Square Berry-466 . . . . 12.00-14.00
Nappy-483 . . . . 8.00-10.00
Vase-555 . . . . 8.00-10.00
Nappy-5316A 9.00-11.00
Berry-532A 8.00-10.00
Oval Dish-538 . . . . 6.00-8.00
Jelly-537 . . . . 6.00-8.00
Mayonnaise & Plate Set-555 . . . . 14.00-16.00

Page 146

Flip Vase-742 . . . . 8.00-10.00
Ivy Ball-Footed-742 . . . . 8.00-10.00
Ivy Ball & Chain-7243 . . . . 10.00-12.00
Square Nappy-7415B 4.00-5.00
Cologne & Stopper-7426 . . . . 26.00-34.00
Cologne & Stopper-742 . . . . 10.00-11.00
Puff Box & Cover-742 . . . . 9.00-10.00

Page 147

Tumbler-741 . . . . 4.00-5.00
Pitcher-741 . . . . 16.00-18.00
Salad Plate-742 . . . . 3.00-4.00
Ice Tea-7412 . . . . 4.00-5.00
Goblet-742 . . . . 3.00-4.00
Sherbet-742 . . . . 3.00-4.00
Salad Plate-Square-7415D 5.00-6.00

Page 148

Salad Plate-1655D	3.00-4.00
Goblet-165	4.00-5.00
Sherbet-165	2.00-3.00
Iced Tea-165	3.00-4.00
Ice Pitcher-Lipped-165	12.00-14.00
Nappy-1655W	2.00-3.00
Finger Bowl-1654 ½ A	3.00-4.00
Baked Apple-1654 ½ X	3.00-4.00
Nappy-1655F	3.00-4.00
Plate-1664 ½ D	2.00-3.00
Baked Apple-1664 ½ X	2.00-3.00
Nappy-1664 ½ W	2.00-3.00
Compote-166	3.00-4.00
Flower Bowl-1346N	4.00-5.00
Finger Bowl-1664 ½ A	2.00-3.00
Sherbet & Plate Set-166	3.00-4.00
Cocktail Glass-166	1.00-2.00
Water Glass-166	1.00-2.00
Ice Tea-166	1.00-2.00
Mug-134	3.00-4.00
Compote or Pretzel-1346A	5.00-7.00

Page 149

Plate-L4736D	3.00-4.00
Plate-L4738D	5.00-6.00
Bowl-L4738F	4.00-5.00
Finger Bowl-L4735J	2.00-3.00
Lunch Tray-L473	6.00-7.00
Fruit Tray-L4731	6.00-7.00
Cup & Saucer-L473	4.00-5.00
Goblet-L473	2.00-3.00
Tumbler-L473	2.00-3.00
Pitcher-L473	9.00-11.00
Wine-L473	2.00-3.00
Decanter & Stopper-L473	6.00-8.00

Page 150

Vase-L473	8.00-10.00
Basket-L473	15.00-18.00
Compote-L473C	6.00-7.00
Lily Bowl-L4736N	5.00-6.00
Bowl-L4736A	3.00-4.00
Nappy-L4736F	3.00-4.00
Bowl-L4736B	4.00-5.00
Fruit-L4735A	3.00-4.00
Fruit-L4735	5.00-6.00
Nappy-L4735B	3.00-4.00
Nappy-L4738B	5.00-6.00

Page 151

Tray-153/1	5.00-7.00
Plate-6998D	4.00-6.00
Torte Plate-592	3.00-4.00
Torte Plate-4140F	5.00-6.00
Plate-72710/4D	7.00-8.00
Birthday Cake Plate-72	15.00-20.00

Page 152

Marmalade Set-169	6.00-8.00
Canape Set-142	7.00-9.00
Cigarette Set-785/3	10.00-12.00
Ash Tray-451	2.00-3.00
Tumbler-760	1.50-2.00
Cocktail Set-85	20.00-25.00
Cup & Plate (Single)	2.00-3.00
Iced Tea Set-1550	20.00-25.00

Page 153

Orange Bowl-6996W	10.00-12.00
Tidbit Set-699	12.00-14.00
Candlestick-765	8.00-10.00
Salt-699	3.00-4.00
Fruit Bowl-6999W	4.00-6.00
Custard-669	2.00-2.50
Celery Tray-699	5.00-6.00
Lily or Nut Bowl-6997N	4.00-5.00
Pitcher-6996	8.00-9.00
Ice Jug-6995	14.00-18.00
Pitcher-6994	8.00-9.00
Lily or Nut Bowl-6996N	4.00-5.00

Page 154

Goblet-6992	3.00-4.00
Sherbet-6992	3.00-4.00
Cocktail-699B	3.00-4.00
Wine-699	3.00-4.00
Old Fashioned-699	3.50-4.50
Iced Tea-699	3.00-4.00
Table Tumbler-699	3.00-4.00
Bon Bon-699	2.00-3.00
Pickle Tray-699	4.00-5.00
Nappy-6991	4.00-5.00
Cup & Saucer-6992	2.00-3.00
Finger Bowl-6994	2.00-3.00
Bread & Butter-6993D	2.00-3.00
Plate-6990D	3.00-4.00
Square Plate-6995D	3.00-4.00
Open Sugar-6990	2.00-3.00
Cream-6990	2.00-3.00
Ice or Butter Tub-6991W	6.00-7.00
Torte Plate-69910F	5.00-7.00
Cake Plate-6997D	4.00-6.00
Sandwich Plate-6998D	5.00-7.00

Page 155

Bitters Bottle-323	6.00-7.00
Cocktail Shaker-142	18.00-22.00
Decanter-625	10.00-12.00
Ice Tub-84	8.00-10.00
Canape Set-158	5.00-6.00

Continued on Page 14

Continued from Page 13

Canape Set-142 . . . . .6.00-8.00
Boot Whiskey-100 .5.00-7.00
Cocktail Glass-142 . . . . .1.00-2.00
Ash Tray-451 . . . . .1.00-2.00
Old Fashioned-658 . . . . .3.00-4.00
Old Fashioned-160 . . . . .3.00-4.00
Old Fashioned-756 . . . . .3.00-4.00
Old Fashioned-699 . . . . .4.00-5.00
Vase-451 7 ½ " 2.00-3.00
Vase-4512 . . . . .2.00-3.00
Vase-451 9 ½ " 3.00-4.00
Rose Bowl-4512 . . . . .3.00-4.00
Liquor-355 . . . . .1.00-2.00
Decanter-3551 . . . . .6.00-8.00
Tumbler-355 . . . . .1.50-2.00
Jug-355 . . . . .8.00-9.00
Decanter-451 . . . . .10.00-12.00
Cocktail Shaker-451 . . . . .18.00-20.00
Ice Pitcher-451 . . . . .8.00-9.00
Tumbler-451 . . . . .1.00-2.00
Tumbler-451 9 ¾ oz. 2.00-2.50
Tumbler-451 5 ½ oz. 2.00-3.00
Liquor-451 2 ½ oz. 1.00-2.00
Finger Bowl-144 . . . . .2.00-3.00
Tumbler-451 5 oz. .2.00-3.00
Tumbler-451 9 oz. .2.50-3.00
Tumbler-451 12 oz. 2.00-3.00
Cordial-451 . . . . .3.00-4.00
Wine-451 . . . . .3.00-3.50
Oyster-451 . . . . .3.00-3.50
Cocktail-451 . . . . .2.00-2.50
Low Sherbet-451 .2.00-3.00
Tall Sherbet-451 . . . . .2.00-3.00
Goblet-451 . . . . .2.50-3.00

Page 156

Nappy-7455B 3.00-4.00
Rose Bowl-780Z 5.00-6.00
Square Compote-780S 5.00-6.00
Vase-780K 5.00-6.00
Compote-780W 6.00-7.00
Vase-743B 5.00-7.00
Vase-743N 5.00-7.00
Vase-743K 5.00-7.00
Nappy-7455F 4.00-5.00
Bowl-7432B 4.50-6.00
Nappy-7805F 3.50-4.50
Plate-7455D 3.00-4.00
Nappy7432F 4.00-5.00
Plate-7432D 4.00-5.00
Sweet Pea-7805K .5.00-6.00
Square Nappy-7805S 5.00-6.00
Plate-7805D 3.00-4.00
Ensemble-749/1 .14.00-16.00
Rose Bowl 4.00-5.00

Flower Holder .1.00-2.00
Candlestick (Single) 3.00-4.00
Plate 2.00-3.00
Ensemble-749/2 . . . . .14.00-16.00
Rose Bowl 4.00-5.00
Flower Holder .1.00-2.00
Candlestick (Single) 3.00-4.00
Plate 2.00-3.00
Ivy Ball with Chain-745 . . . . .10.00-12.00
Deep Bowl-7805W 3.00-4.00
Compote-761 . . . . .5.00-7.00
Tid Bit Set-7432/86 . . . . .9.00-11.00
Tid Bit Set-7498/87 . . . . .9.00-11.00

Page 157

Plate-7499D 5.00-8.00
Orange Bowl-7499B 6.00-8.00
Fruit Bowl-7499F .6.00-8.00
Flower Bowl-7499N 4.00-5.00
Flower Bowl & Holder-7498R 4.00-5.00
Flower Bowl & Holder-7498K 5.00-6.00
Flower Bowl-7498N 5.00-6.00
Plate-7497D 3.00-5.00
Basket Bowl-7497E 6.00-8.00
Bowl-7498B 4.00-6.00
Bowl-7497F 3.00-5.00
Rose Bowl & Holder-7497K 4.00-6.00
Flower Bowl & Holder-7497R 4.00-6.00
Plate-7498D 4.00-6.00
Bowl-7497B 3.00-5.00
Flower Bowl-7497N 3.00-4.00
Rose Bowl & Holder-1346N 4.00-6.00
Blown Rose Bowl-770/2 . . . . .5.00-7.00
Bowl-7498F 3.00-4.00

Page 158

Punch Set-SNAP-14 . . . . .50.00-60.00
Punch Set-60020 .40.00-50.00
Punch Set-46420 .70.00-90.00
Glass Ladle-91 . . . . .8.00-10.00
Punch Set-70020 .45.00-60.00
Punch Set-16010 .50.00-60.00
Punch Set-69810 .50.00-60.00
Punch Set-700 . . . . .55.00-70.00

Page 159

Console Set-7499B 12.00-15.00
Console Set-1537 .14.00-16.00
Console Set-7499F 12.00-15.00
Console Set-648B/169 . . . . .14.00-16.00
Console Set-7498B 12.00-15.00
Console Set-153B .16.00-18.00
Console Set-7498F 14.00-16.00
Console Set-6567/169 . . . . .16.00-18.00
Console Set-7497B 12.00-14.00
Console Set-7497F 14.00-16.00

Page 160

Goblet-160	4.00-5.00
Sherbet-160	2.00-3.00
Cocktail-160B	3.00-4.00
Ice Tea-160	3.00-4.00
Ginger Ale-160	3.00-4.00
Old Fashion-160	3.00-4.00
Wine-160	3.00-4.00
Whiskey-160	3.00-4.00
Plate-1604½D	2.00-3.00
Salad Plate-1605D	3.00-4.00
Cup & Saucer-160	3.00-4.00
Jelly-1601W	2.00-3.00
Fruit-1604W	2.00-3.00
Baked Apple Nappy-1604½X	3.00-4.00
Decanter & Stopper-160	9.00-10.00
Mayonnaise Set-1605	6.00-8.00
Flared Nappy-1605W	3.00-4.00
Shallow Nappy-1605F	3.00-4.00
Finger Bowl-1604½A	2.00-3.00
Coaster-1601R	2.00-3.00
Sugar & Cream Set-160	6.00-8.00
Compote-160F	5.00-6.00
Compote-160X	5.00-6.00
Divided Relish-160U	6.00-8.00

Page 161

Fruit-1604½X	3.00-4.00
Finger Bowl-1604½	3.00-4.00
Custard Cup-160	2.00-3.00
Coaster-1601	2.00-3.00
Fruit Nappy-1604W	2.00-3.00
Fruit Bowl-1605W	3.00-4.00
Cup & Saucer-160	3.50-4.50
Shallow Nappy-1605F	4.00-5.00

Page 162

Salad Plate-1604½D	3.00-4.00
Mayonnaise Set-1608	8.00-9.00
Buffet-16010	9.00-10.00
Salad Plate-1605D	3.00-4.00
Fruit Bowl-16010B	6.00-8.00
Salad Bowl-16010A	5.00-6.00
Salad Plate-6985D	3.00-4.00
Center Bowl-16010R	5.00-6.00
Buffet-69810	9.00-11.00
Mayonnaise Set-1605	6.00-8.00
Tid Bit Set-698	8.00-10.00
Vase-698	6.00-9.00
Square Salad Set-698	6.00-8.00

Page 163

Goblet-698	3.00-5.00
Cocktail-698	3.00-5.00
Sherbet-698	3.00-5.00
Bread & Butter Plate-6983D	2.00-3.00
Salad Plate-6980D	2.00-3.00
Dinner Plate-6981D	3.00-4.00
Coaster	2.00-3.00
Water Tumbler-698	2.00-3.00
Ice Tea-698	3.00-4.00
Cup & Saucer-6982	4.00-5.00
Open Sugar-6980	3.00-4.00
Creamer-6980	3.00-4.00
Cream Soup-698	3.00-4.00
Butter Tub-6981W	5.00-6.00
Oval Pickle Dish-698	3.00-4.00
Oval Celery Tray-698	3.00-4.00
Mayonnaise Set-698	4.00-6.00
Round Vegetable-6981W	3.00-4.00
Bon Bon-698	3.00-4.00
Finger Bowl-698	2.00-3.00
Covered Cheese Dish-698	12.00-15.00
Salt & Pepper Set-698	3.00-4.00
Compote-698X	3.00-6.00
Compote-698F	3.00-6.00

Page 164

Lily Bowl-6988N	5.00-6.00
Lily Bowl-6987N	4.00-6.00
Lily Bowl-6986N	3.00-5.00
Lily Bowl-6985N	2.00-4.00
Ice Lip Pitcher-6988	10.00-12.00
Round Plate-6988D	3.00-4.00
Round Plate-6987D	3.00-4.00
Square Plate-698	3.00-4.00
Square Bowl-698	3.00-4.00
Vase-6981	6.00-9.00
Vase-6982	4.00-6.00
Flower Bowl-6987N	3.00-5.00
Basket-698	9.00-12.00
Divided Relish-698	5.00-7.00

Page 165

Ice Tea Set-701.1	14.00-16.00
Sugar & Cream Set-701	8.00-10.00
Ash Tray-701	3.00-3.50
Fruit-7014F	2.00-2.50
Deep Salad Bowl-7018B	8.00-10.00
Plate-7018D	3.00-4.00
Nappy-7016W	3.00-4.00
Salad Plate-7016D	2.00-3.00
Cup & Saucer-701	2.00-3.00
Ball Console Set-701/2	10.00-12.00
Vanity Set-701	10.00-12.00
Plate-7018V	3.00-4.00

Page 166

Ice Lip Pitcher-701	10.00-12.00
Ice Tea-701.1	1.00-2.00
Hiball-701	1.00-2.00
Juice-701	1.00-2.00
Cocktail-Footed-701	1.00-2.00

Continued on Page 16

Continued from Page 15

Old Fashioned-701 . . . . .1.00-2.00
Ball-701/5 . . . . .2.00-3.00
Ball-701/6 . . . . .3.00-4.00
Rose Bowl-701/2 . . . . .4.00-5.00
Bud Vase-701/3 . . . . .3.00-4.00
Bitters-701 . . . . .5.00-6.00
Cigarette Holder-701 . . . . .4.00-5.00
Candleholder-701 . . . . .6.00-7.00
Cocktail Shaker 9.00-12.00
Rose Bowl-701/1 . . . . .5.00-6.00
Vase-701/4 . . . . .5.00-6.00
Old Fashion-701 . . . . .4.00-5.00
Ice Tub-701 . . . . .5.00-6.00
Muddler-701 . . . . .3.00-4.00
Cigarette Set-701 . . . . .5.00-6.00
Ball Smoker-701 . . . . .4.00-5.00
Cocktail Set-701/4F 14.00-20.00

Page 167

Plate-7799D 3.00-4.00
Square Plate-779S 3.00-4.00
Cupped Plate-7799V 3.50-5.00
Flared Bowl-7799W 4.00-5.00
Flower Bowl-7799N 3.00-4.00
Lily Bowl-7796N 3.00-4.00
Individual Salt-779 . . . . .2.00-3.00
Round Tray-779 . . . . .4.00-6.00
Plate-7796D 3.00-4.00
Round Bowl-7796A 2.00-3.00
Fancy Square Bowl-7796S 4.00-6.00
Flared Bowl-7796W 3.00-4.00
Candleholder-7796 . . . . .4.00-6.00

Page 168

Cologne-779 . . . . .5.00-8.00
Flower Bowl-7796N 4.00-6.00
Square Vase-779S 6.00-7.00
Candy Box & Cover-779 . . . . .6.00-8.00
Square Cologne-699 . . . . .5.00-8.00
Fancy Bowl-779SC 4.00-6.00
Oval Divided Relish-779 . . . . .4.00-6.00
Square Salad Set-779S 5.00-8.00
Square Bowl 3.00-5.00
Square Fruit-779S 2.00-3.00
Ash Tray-7792 .1.00-2.00
Ash Receiver-779 . . . . .2.00-3.00
Mayonnaise Set-779S 5.00-7.00
Square Candlestick-779 . . . . .6.00-9.00
Square Plate-779S 2.00-3.00
Canape Set-779 . . . . .3.00-4.00
Console Set-779S 10.00-15.00

Page 169

Salad Set-400/51340 . . . . .45.00-55.00
    Salad Plate-400/5D 2.00-3.00
    Mayonnaise set-400/40 . . . . .5.00-7.00
    Salad Set-400/13FD 6.00-8.00

Luncheon Set-400/13 . . . . .50.00-60.00
    Salad Plate-400/5D 2.00-3.00
    Cup & Saucer-400/35 . . . . .3.00-4.00
    Sugar-400/31 . . . . .2.00-3.00
    Plate-400/13D 4.00-6.00
    Cream-400/31 . . . . .2.00-3.00

Page 170

Compote-400/66B 3.00-4.00
Compote-400/63B 3.00-4.00
Cheese & Cracker-400/88 . . . . .6.00-7.00
Canape Set-400/36 . . . . .6.00-7.00
Vase Fan Shape-400/87F 4.00-6.00
Vase-400/87R .4.00-6.00
Mayonnaise Set-400/40 . . . . .6.00-7.00
Nappy-400/74B 3.00-5.00
Candleholder-400-86 . . . . .2.00-3.00
Candleholder-400-81 . . . . .4.00-5.00
Ash Tray-400/34 . . . . .2.00-3.00
Dish-400/74SC 4.00-6.00
Lily Bowl-400/74J 4.00-6.00
Candlestick-400/80 . . . . .3.00-4.00
Cake Stand-400/67D 7.00-9.00
Center Bowl-400/13B 5.00-7.00
Footed Bowl-400/67B 5.00-7.00

Page 171

Octagon Luncheon Set-56 . . . . .50.00-60.00
    Plate-7275D 2.00-3.00
    Cup & Saucer-725/2 . . . . .3.00-4.00
    Sugar-725/6 . . . . .2.00-3.00
    Tray-7257D 6.00-8.00
    Cream-725/6 . . . . .2.00-3.00
    Salad Plate-7285D 2.00-3.00
Square Luncheon Set-7608 . . . . .50.00-60.00
    Plate-7875D 2.00-3.00
    Cup & Saucer-760 . . . . .3.00-4.00
    Sugar-760 . . . . .2.00-3.00
    Tray-7608D 5.00-6.00
    Cream-760 . . . . .2.00-3.00
    Salad Plate-7885D 2.00-3.00

Page 172

Sugar & Cream Set-682 . . . . .4.00-6.00
Bouquet-682 . . . . .4.00-5.00
Oval Celery Tray-682 . . . . .3.00-5.00
Shallow Compote-682F 4.00-5.00
Mayonnaise Set-682B 3.00-5.00
Flared Bowl-6820W 3.50-4.50
Square Plate-682S 2.00-4.00
Square Dish-628S 2.00-4.00
Belled Nappy-6825B 3.00-4.00
Two-handled Pickle-682 . . . . .4.00-5.00
Two-Handled Jelly-682 . . . . .4.00-5.00

Continued on Page 17

Continued from Page 16

One-Handled Nappy-682 . . . . .2.00-3.00
Bon Bon-6825C 3.00-5.00
Two-Handled Partitioned Relish-682/2 . . . .4.00-5.00
Compote-682B 4.00-5.00
Flower Bowl-6825N 3.00-4.00

Page 173
Luncheon Set-6828D 55.00-65.00
    Cake Plate-6828D 4.00-5.00
    Cup & Saucer-682 . . . . .3.00-5.00
    Salad Plate-6820D 2.00-3.00
    Sugar & Cream 4.00-6.00
Salad Bowl-6828B .5.00-7.00
Salad Bowl-6827B .4.00-6.00
Plate-6827D 3.00-4.00
Console Set-153B 18.00-20.00
Plate-6823D 2.00-3.00

Page 174
Serving Set-7888/3D 45.00-50.00
    Square Plate-7888/3D 8.00-10.00
    Square Plate-7885/3D 6.00-8.00
    Bowl-7257/3F 8.00-10.00
    Plate-7257/3D 10.00-12.00
    Bowl-5889F/99 . . . . .8.00-10.00
    Bulb Bowl-5889 NC/99 . . . . .9.00-10.00
    Relish Dish-5889/99 . . . . .9.00-11.00
    Salad Bowl-7257/3W 8.00-10.00
    Tray-5889C/99 . . . . .8.00-10.00
    Plate-7497/3D 10.00-12.00
    Belled Bowl-7497/3B 10.00-12.00
    Shallow Bowl-7497/3F 10.00-12.00

Page 175
Fruit Bowl-7499/4F 10.00-12.00
Relish-265 . . . . .8.00-10.00
Nappy-7436/5F 8.00-10.00
Cup & Saucer-900 . . . . .12.00-14.00
Orange Bowl-7499/4B 10.00-12.00
Crescent Salad Plate-736 . . . . .8.00-10.00
Plate-7436/5D 8.00-10.00
Square Salad Plate-698/5 . . . . .12.00-14.00
Plate-7499D 12.00-14.00
Cabaret Plate-7499/4V 12.00-14.00
Coaster-600/4 . . . . .4.00-6.00
Square Salad Bowl-698/5 . . . . .6.00-8.00
Bowl-7436/5B 8.00-10.00
Salad Set-255/50X 14.00-16.00
Round Bowl-255/5A 8.00-10.00
Fruit Bowl-255/5 .8.00-10.00
Plate-255/5D 6.00-8.00

Page 176
Ash Tray-785 . . . . .4.00-6.00
Cigarette Box-785 . . . . .14.00-16.00
Salad Plate-800 .8.00-10.00
Shallow Nappy-900 . . . . .6.00-8.00

Shallow Fruit Bowl-900 . . . . .10.00-12.00
Salad Plate-900 . . . . .8.00-10.00
Torte or Chop Plate-900 . . . . .10.00-12.00

Page 177
Nappy-L7255/4B .8.00-10.00
Mayonnaise Set-L7255/4 . . . . .14.00-16.00
Bowl-L7258/4W .10.00-12.00
Bowl-L7258/4F 10.00-12.00
Fruit Bowl-L72710/4A 14.00-16.00
Nappy-L7275/4F .8.00-10.00
Plate-L7255/4D 8.00-10.00
Salad Plate-L7275/4D 8.00-10.00
Torte Plate-L72710/4D 16.00-18.00
Plate-L7258/4D .14.00-16.00

Page 178
Plate-L6028D 12.00-14.00
Bowl-L6025B 6.00-8.00
Bowl-L6028B 8.00-10.00
Nappy-L6025F 7.00-9.00
Bowl-L6025F 10.00-12.00
Plate-L6025D 8.00-10.00
Nappy-L900 . . . . .7.00-9.00
Shallow Bowl-L900 . . . . .12.00-14.00
Relish Tray-7480 . . . . .12.00-14.00
Plate-14"-L900 .16.00-18.00
Plate-10½"-L900 . . . . .14.00-16.00
Plate-8"L900 . . . . .10.00-12.00
Relish Tray-748 .13.00-15.00
Relish Set-783 . . . . .12.00-14.00

Page 179
Plate-85 . . . . .10.00-12.00
Plate-592 . . . . .10.00-12.00
Plate-2428 . . . . .8.00-10.00
Soup Bowl-85 . . . . .4.00-6.00
Relish Tray-78 . . . . .8.00-10.00
Baked Apple-85 . . . . .6.00-8.00
Salt & Pepper-760 . . . . .4.00-6.00
Cocktail Set-46 .12.00-14.00

Page 180
Basket-300 (3) ea. 10.00-12.00
Salad Set-255/5 .8.00-10.00
Cake Plate-255/5D 6.00-8.00
Console Set-0/378/75 . . . . .18.00-20.00
Night Set-805 (3) ea. 8.00-10.00
Console Set-75BX/42 . . . . .18.00-20.00
Bud Vase-451 (3) ea. 4.00-6.00

Page 181
Sandwich Tray-728 . . . . .6.00-8.00
Compote-7286A 6.00-9.00
Bowl-7257W 6.00-8.00
Footed Plate-7286D 4.00-6.00
Rose Bowl-7286Y .4.00-6.00
Mayonnaise & Ladle-723R 5.00-7.00

Continued on Page 18

17

Continued from Page 17

Candy Box & Cover-716 . . . . .8.00-10.00
Plate-7257D 3.00-5.00

Page 182

Sandwich Tray-664 . . . . .6.00-8.00
Bowl-6153B 5.00-7.00
Fruit Bowl-647W 4.00-5.00
Basket-300 .8.00-10.00
Oval Celery Tray-6150 . . . . .3.00-5.00
Preserve-84B 4.00-6.00
Vase-244B 5.00-8.00
Sugar, Cream & Tray Set-1693 . . . . .10.00-12.00

Page 183

Tumbler-5 ½ oz.-451 . . . . .1.50-2.00
Tumbler-9 ¾ oz.-451 . . . . .2.00-2.50
Tumbler-12 ½ oz.-451 . . . . .2.50-3.00
Ice Pitcher-451 . . . . .8.00-10.00
Salad Plate-2427 ½ 3.00-4.00
Goblet-250 . . . . .4.00-5.00
Saucer Champagne-250 . . . . .3.00-5.00
Cocktail-250 .2.00-4.00

Page 184

Plate-85 . . . . .6.00-8.00
Salad Plate-2428 . . . . .4.00-5.00
Compote-169 . . . . .4.00-5.00
Relish Tray-78 . . . . .5.00-7.00
Covered Box-757 . . . . .8.00-10.00
Plate-592 . . . . .6.00-8.00
Console Set-75X 15.00-18.00
Console Set-320 . . . . .15.00-18.00

Page 185

Lily Bowl-7615N 4.00-5.00
Nappy-7615 .4.00-5.00
Bon Bon Tray-7251 . . . . .5.00-7.00
Nappy-7275W 3.00-5.00
Plate-7255D .3.00-5.00
Nappy-7255W 4.00-6.00
Square Nappy-7605W 4.00-6.00
Bud Vase-6923 . . . . .6.00-8.00
Rose Bowl-7286Y 3.00-5.00
Comport-7286A 4.00-6.00
Mayonnaise & Ladle-723R 4.00-6.00
Bowl-7257W 5.00-7.00
Plate-7286D .3.00-4.00
Candy Box & Cover-716 . . . . .8.00-10.00
Plate-7257D .5.00-7.00
Sandwich Tray-728 . . . . .7.00-9.00

Page 186

Mayonnaise Set-450 . . . . .6.00-8.00
Goblet-450 . . . . .3.00-4.00
Tall Sherbet-450 . . . . .2.50-3.00
Tumbler-12 oz.-450 . . . . .3.00-4.00
Tumbler-9 oz.-450 . . . . .2.50-3.00

Tumbler-5 oz.-450 . . . . .2.00-2.50
Plate-7230 . . . . .2.00-3.00
Cordial-450 .2.00-3.00
Wine-450 . . . . .2.50-3.50
Cocktail-450 .2.50-3.50
Finger Bowl-450 . . . . .3.00-4.00
Low Sherbet-450 . . . . .3.00-4.00
Plate-499 . . . . .2.00-3.00
Oval Console Bowl-320 . . . . .8.00-10.00
Console Set-75BX 18.00-20.00
Console Set-734 . . . . .18.00-20.00

Page 187

Bowl-7257W 8.00-10.00
Sugar, Cream & Tray Set-7723 . . . . .14.00-16.00
Relish Plate-78 . . . . .8.00-10.00
Plate-7257D .8.00-10.00
Lunch Tray-760/2 . . . . .10.00-12.00
Covered Dish-724 . . . . .10.00-12.00
Cake Plate-7287D 10.00-12.00
Compote-7287A 6.00-8.00
Cheese & Cracker Set-727 . . . . .8.00-10.00
Relish Tray-728 . . . . .6.00-8.00
Celery Tray-727 . . . . .5.00-7.00
Mayonnaise Set-7255W 8.00-10.00
Relish Dish-761 . . . . .9.00-10.00
Supper Plate-592 . . . . .4.00-6.00
Deep Bowl-378 . . . . .5.00-7.00

Page 188

Plate-6''-2426 . . . . .2.00-2.50
Plate-7 ½ ''-2427 ½ 2.50-3.00
Plate-10 ½ ''-24210 . . . . .3.00-4.00
Plate-6''-72/1 . . . . .2.0-2.50
Plate-8''-72/4 . . . . .3.00-3.50
Plate-15''-72/8 . . . . .4.00-5.00
Belled Nappy-7 ½ ''-85 . . . . .4.00-6.00
Belled Nappy-6 ½ ''-85 . . . . .3.00-5.00
Salt & Pepper-760 . . . . .4.00-5.00
Ice Cube Set-35 . . . . .10.00-12.00

Page 189

Sugar & Cream Set-760 . . . . .10.00-12.00
Mayonnaise Set-727 . . . . .8.00-10.00
Vase-727 . . . . .6.00-8.00
Compote-7286W 5.00-6.00
Bon Bon Tray-7251/1 . . . . .6.00-8.00
Rose Bowl-7286Y 6.00-8.00
Covered Dish-724 . . . . .10.00-12.00
Celery Tray-727/1 . . . . .6.00-8.00

Page 190

Mayonnaise Set-7255W 8.00-10.00
Cake Plate-10 ½ ''-7257D 8.00-10.00
Cake Plate-13''-72510D 6.00-8.00
Bowl-7257W 6.00-8.00
Sugar, Cream & Tray Set-7723 . . . . .14.00-16.00
Cracker & Cheese Set-727 . . . . .8.00-10.00

Page 191

Console Set-734W	25.00-30.00
Console Set-320/1	18.00-20.00
Console Set-320/2	28.00-32.00
Console Set-7287A	18.00-20.00

Page 192

Blown Vase-153	8.00-10.00
Goblet-250	4.00-5.00
Saucer Champagne-250	3.00-4.00
Cocktail-250	2.00-3.00
Covered Candy Box-757/1	10.00-12.00
Covered Candy Box-757/2	10.00-12.00
Square Sandwich Tray-760/2	10.00-12.00

Page 193

Beverage Set-(7)-451	20.00-25.00
Beverage Set-(9)-451	20.00-25.00
(All Cuts)	

Page 194

Relish-727/2	6.00-8.00
Bon Bon Tray-7251/1	6.00-8.00
Candy Box & Cover-716	8.00-10.00
Preserve-727W	4.00-6.00
Lily Bowl-7615N	7.00-9.00
Nappy-7615B	7.00-9.00
Bowl-7255W	5.00-7.00
Plate-7255D	4.00-6.00
Goblet-250	5.00-6.00
Tall Sherbet-250	4.00-5.00
Low Sherbet-250	3.00-4.00
Cocktail-250	2.00-3.00
Tumbler-5 ½ oz.-250	2.00-3.00
Tumbler-9 oz.-250	3.00-4.00
Tumbler-12 oz.-250	3.50-4.50

Page 195

Sandwich Tray-728	10.00-12.00
Sugar & Cream Set-760	10.00-12.00
Relish Tray-727	8.00-10.00
Covered Box-757/2	10.00-12.00
Compote-169	8.00-10.00
Rose Bowl-4512	5.00-7.00
Bowl-7257W	6.00-8.00
Mayonnaise Set-7255W	8.00-10.00

Page 196

Sugar & Cream Set-760	10.00-12.00
Sandwich Tray-728	10.00-12.00
Relish Tray-727/2	8.00-10.00
Bon Bon Tray-7251/1	6.00-8.00
Bowl-7257W	6.00-8.00
Compote-7286W	5.00-7.00
Celery Tray-727/1	6.00-8.00
Covered Nut Box-724/2	10.00-12.00
Salt & Pepper Set-760	4.00-5.00
Mayonnaise Set-7255W	8.00-10.00
Rose Bowl-7286Y	6.00-8.00
Cake Plate-7257D	6.00-8.00

Page 197

Lunch Tray-760/2	10.00-12.00
Sugar, Cream & Tray Set-7723	14.00-16.00
Rose Bowl-7287Y	6.00-8.00
Tall Compote-169	8.00-10.00
Cheese & Crackers Set-727	8.00-10.00
Compote-7287A	5.00-7.00
Mayonnaise Set-727/9	8.00-10.00
Covered Candy Box-757/2	10.00-12.00
Marmalade Set-169	8.00-10.00

Page 198

Console Set-75X	18.00-20.00
Console Set-320/75	20.00-22.00
Console Set-734A/75	18.00-20.00
Console Set-648B/637D	15.00-18.00
Partitioned Relish Plate-78	8.00-10.00
Torte Plate-85	8.00-10.00
Torte Plate-592	8.00-10.00

Page 199

Square Lunch Tray-10/760/2	10.00-12.00
Bowl-10/7257W	8.00-10.00
Candy Box & Cover-10/717	12.00-14.00
Sugar & Cream Set-10/760	10.00-12.00
Cake Plate-10/7257D	8.00-10.00
Mayonnaise Set-10/7255W	8.00-10.00
Rose Bowl-10/7287Y	6.00-8.00
Console Set-10/7287X/728	18.00-22.00

Page 200

Rose Bowl-7801Z	6.00-8.00
Bon Bon-7801S	6.00-8.00
Vase-7801K	6.00-8.00
Compote-7801W	8.00-10.00
Plate-7802D	3.00-4.00
Shallow Nappy-7802F	3.00-4.00
Belled Nappy-7802B	3.50-4.50
Vase-7803K	6.00-8.00
Vase-7803N	6.00-8.00
Vase-7803B	6.00-8.00
Compote-761	5.00-7.00
Candlestick-677	8.00-10.00
Nappy-7615B	7.00-9.00
Bon Bon Tray-7251/1	6.00-8.00
Nappy-7745W	5.00-7.00
Lily Bowl-7615N	7.00-9.00

Page 201

Vase-743K	5.00-8.00
Vase-743N	5.00-8.00
Vase-743X	5.00-8.00
Vase-743B	5.00-8.00
Chicken-on-Nest-145	6.00-10.00
Plate-7455D	3.00-5.00
Basket Bowl-7455G	3.00-5.00
Belled Nappy-7455B	3.00-5.00
Shallow Nappy-7455F	4.00-7.00

Page 202

Tumblers:

Lamp-1748/13	4.00-6.00
Elephant-1748/14	4.00-6.00
Mouse-1748/15	4.00-6.00
Parrot-1748/16	4.00-6.00
Duck-1748/17	4.00-6.00
Rabbit-1748/18	4.00-6.00
Cat-1748/19	4.00-6.00
Turtle-1748/20	4.00-6.00
Ape-1748/21	4.00-6.00
Crow-1748/22	4.00-6.00
Lady Bug-1748/23	4.00-6.00
Rooster-1748/24	4.00-6.00
Tomato-103/86	5.00-6.00
Red Rooster-103/85	5.00-6.00
Orange-103/87	5.00-6.00
Happy Hour-8701	8.00-10.00

Page 203

Wine/Liquor Set-451	15.00-20.00
Rose Bowl-4512	4.00-6.00
Tumbler-5 ½ oz.-451	2.00-3.00
Tumbler-9 ¾ oz.-451	2.50-3.00
Tumbler-12 ½ oz.-451	3.00-3.50
Pitcher-451	8.00-10.00

Page 204

Swan-147	15.00-18.00
Honey Pot-60	14.00-20.00
Holder-739	12.00-14.00
Tumbler-7112	3.00-4.00
Tumbler-741	3.00-4.00
Twin Candle Holder-153	8.00-10.00
Belled Console/Fruit Bowl-153B	8.00-12.00

Page 205

Nappy-5885A	6.00-8.00
Tray-5886C	6.00-8.00
Bowl-5887W	6.00-8.00
Tray-5887V	7.00-9.00
Relish-5886	6.00-8.00
Bon Bon-5885B	6.00-8.00
Lily Bowl-5885N	7.00-9.00
Bowl-5886F	7.00-9.00
Muffin-5887H	8.00-10.00
Bowl-5887F	7.00-9.00
Bulb Bowl-5889NC	8.00-10.00
Relish Dish-5889	9.00-11.00
Plate-5887D	8.00-10.00
Tray-5889C	8.00-10.00
Bowl-5889F	8.00-10.00
Bowl-5887B	8.00-10.00

Page 206

Plate-8 ½ "-85	3.00-4.00
Cup & Saucer-242/2	4.00-6.00
Relish Tray-7B	6.00-8.00

Covered Box-757/1	8.00-10.00
Covered Box-757/2	8.00-10.00
Sugar-Cream & Tray Set-7723	14.00-16.00
Cocktail Set-46	12.00-14.00
Cream Soup-231/5	3.00-6.00
Soup-85X	3.00-4.00
Baked Apple-85X	3.00-4.00

Page 207

Console Set-7287A/728	18.00-20.00
Bowl-7287A	8.00-10.00
Candleholder-728 (Pr.)	8.00-12.00
Vase-727	7.00-9.00
Partitioned Relish Tray-727/2	6.00-8.00
Cream-725/8	5.00-6.00
Celery Tray-727/1	6.00-8.00
Sugar & Cream Set-725/8	8.00-10.00
Bouquet-728	5.00-7.00

Page 208

High Stem Compote-169	8.00-10.00
Plate-2428	3.00-4.00
Syrup Jug-46	4.00-5.00
Console Set-75X/637D	18.00-20.00
Bowl-75X	8.00-10.00
Candleholder-637D (Pr.)	8.00-10.00

Page 209

Vase-775	8.00-12.00
Vase-7751	10.00-12.00
Vase-488	18.00-22.00
Flower Pot & Saucer-1	6.00-8.00

Page 210

Plate-11/7003/4	6.00-8.00
Crimped Dish-11/4736C	7.00-9.00
Service Plate-11/7007/4	8.00-10.00
Salad Plate-11/7005/4	7.00-9.00

Page 211

Vase-11/7423C	8.00-10.00
Vase-11/743K	6.00-8.00
Vase-11/743N	6.00-8.00
Vase-11/743X	6.00-8.00
Vase-11/743B	6.00-8.00
Cup & Saucer-11/473	6.00-8.00
Covered Preserve-11/54	8.00-10.00
Chicken-on-Nest-11/145	8.00-10.00
Footed Ivy Ball-11/742	7.00-9.00
Covered Cigarette Box-11/7850	8.00-10.00
Card Holder-11/739	6.00-8.00
Comport-11-54	4.00-6.00

Page 212

Vase-11/488	20.00-24.00
Vase-11/4731	16.00-20.00
Basket-11/473	20.00-30.00
Comport-11/473C	10.00-12.00
Nappy-11/700S/4	6.00-8.00